Meanings into Words
Upper-Intermediate
An integrated course for students of English

Workbook

Adrian Doff, Christopher Jones and Keith Mitchell

 CAMBRIDGE
UNIVERSITY PRESS

Published by the Press Syndicate of the University of Cambridge
The Pitt Building, Trumpington Street, Cambridge CB2 1RP
40 West 20th Street, New York, NY 10011-4211, USA
10 Stamford Road, Oakleigh, Melbourne 3166, Australia

© Cambridge University Press 1984

First published 1984
Eleventh printing 1992

Printed in Great Britain
by Scotprint Ltd, Musselburgh, Scotland

ISBN 0 521 28707 3 Workbook
ISBN 0 521 28705 7 Student's Book
ISBN 0 521 28706 5 Teacher's Book
ISBN 0 521 28708 1 Test Book
ISBN 0 521 24464 1 Cassette (Student's Book)
ISBN 0 521 24465 X Cassette (Drills)

MX

Contents

1 **Experience** 4

2 **Appearance** 9

3 **Relating past events** 13

4 **Attitudes and reactions** 17

5 **Duration** 21

   Revision crossword 26

6 **Reporting** 28

7 **Deductions and explanations** 33

8 **Advantages and disadvantages** 38

9 **Clarifying** 42

10 **Wishes and regrets** 47

   Revision crossword 52

11 **Events in sequence** 54

12 **Comparison** 60

13 **Processes** 64

14 **Prediction** 69

15 **News** 74

   Revision crossword 78

This Workbook accompanies *Meaning into Words Upper-Intermediate*, and provides extra written practice in all the main structures which appear in the Student's Book. It can be used as homework or classroom material or for revision.

The Workbook is divided into 15 units, to accompany Student's Book Units 1–15. Each unit contains four or five exercises, usually including a guided composition. The Workbook also contains three Revision crosswords, which occur after Units 5, 10 and 15.

Acknowledgements

The illustrations on pages 9, 10 and 32 are by Keith Howard. The illustration on page 58 is by John Flynn. The drawings on pages 65, 66 and 67 are by Chris Evans. The photographs on page 12 are reproduced by permission of Tony McGee and *The Sunday Times*. The photographs on pages 7 and 63 are reproduced by permission of Barnaby's Picture Library.
Book design by Peter Ducker MSTD

Unit 1   Experience

1   LISTING EXPERIENCES AND ACHIEVEMENTS

Develop the notes below into short paragraphs, listing each person's experiences
and achievements. Begin with the sentences given.

1   *Brenda Gibbons is just the right person for the job.*

....

....

....

....

....

....

Science (university)
Industrial chemist
Two books on oil
Experience on North Sea oil
   rig
Lecturer on energy (University
   of Cambridge, 1980)

2   *The new party leader, Andrew Fife, is a man of
wide and varied experience.*

....

....

....

....

....

....

....

Journalist
Economist
Minister (two governments)
Chancellor of the Exchequer
   (1974–78)
World-wide travel
Many heads of state

3   *At 60, Brian considers that he's not had a very
exciting life so far.*

....

....

....

....

....

Same job (30 years)
Never move house
Go abroad once – day trip,
   Calais 1965
London – three times
Never visit night-club

4

2 ASKING ABOUT EXPERIENCES

Look at the example, and write similar conversations between A and B. B must give brief details about his/her experience.

1 fine/for a parking offence? (speeding)

A: *Have you ever been fined for a parking offence?*

B: *No I haven't, but I have been fined for speeding. They caught me doing 85 mph on the motorway.*

2 steal/wallet? (umbrella)

A: .... *had* ....

B: ....

....

3 trap/in a lift? (toilet)

A: ....

B: ....

....

4 X-ray/chest? (teeth)

A: ....

B: ....

....

5 throw/out of class? (library)

A: ....

B: ....

....

6 mistake/for a rock star? (TV actor/actress)

A: ....

B: ....

....

3 SUPERLATIVES

Look at the example, and write about the other topics in the same way.

1 mean people
The meanest person I've ever met was Jack Davies. He used to walk everywhere rather than pay for the bus.

2 frightening experiences
....
....
....

3 stupid mistakes
....
....
....

4 uncomfortable beds
....
....
....

5 boring jobs
....
....
....

6 funny films
....
....
....

4 BE USED TO

Continue the remarks below with a sentence using (**not**) **used to** + **ing**.

1   The traffic doesn't wake him up at night...
   He's used to sleeping in the street.

2   He's going to find it hard work working on a building site...

   ....

3   She was quite surprised when I gave her some flowers...

   ....

4   He won't mind if you stare at him...

   ....

5   I get a bit lonely sometimes, now that she's gone...

   ....

6   It's quite hard work doing all my own washing and cleaning...

   ....

7   I don't think she's ever opened a door herself...

   ....

8   You can bring as many friends as you like home to dinner...

   ....

9   I'm not surprised he's out of breath...

   ....

10 Ooh dear. I've got a stomach-ache...

   ....

5 HOW MANY TIMES?

Express each of the sentences below in two other ways.

1 I've only visited Britain once before.

   a) *This is only my second visit to Britain.*

   b) *This is only the second time I've visited Britain.*

2 This is my first night in a 5-star hotel.

   a) *I've never slept*

   b) *This is the first time*

3 This is his third stretch in prison.

   a) ....

   b) ....

   ....

4 This is the first time I've worked in a travel agent's.

   a) ....

   b) ....

   ....

5 I've flown in Concorde four times before.

   a) ....

   b) ....

   ....

6 This is only my third attack of flu.

   a) ....

   b) ....

   ....

Unit 2 Appearance

1 JUDGING FROM APPEARANCES

What do the appearances of the people below suggest to you? Write three sentences
for each picture: one with **look** + adjective, two with **look as if/as though**.

a) ....
....

b) ....
....

c) ....
....

a) ....
....

b) ....
....

c) ....
....

a) ....
....

b) ....
....

c) ....
....

>>>→

a) ....
....

b) ....
....

c) ....
....

2 IDENTIFYING WITH 'LIKE'

Continue the following remarks with **look**, **sound**, **smell**, **feel** or **taste**, + **like**.

1 Surely he's not a manual worker...
He looks like a businessman to me.
....

2 Are you sure this is tea?...
....

3 I wonder who wrote that music...
....

4 He's got a foreign accent...
....

5 This material's very soft...
....

6 What's that you're cooking?...
....

7 They've got very similar faces...
....

8 This isn't real leather, is it?...
....

9 I've got something in my shoe...
....

10 I don't think you made this cake yourself...
....

3 IMPRESSIONS: SEEM

The police have found a man unconscious. They don't know who he is, but they
have some ideas about him. From the evidence below, say what impressions the police
have about the man, using **seem**.

He's blond, and his clothes have Swedish labels. He's well dressed,
and is wearing an expensive ring. He has nicotine stains on his
fingers, and some old scars on his face. He's well built, and his
hands are very rough. He has a used plane ticket from Amsterdam
in his pocket, dated four days ago. He was found in the middle of a
park, with a nasty wound at the back of his head.

1 *He seems to be a heavy smoker.*
2 *He doesn't seem to have been robbed.*
3 ....
4 ....
5 ....
6 ....
7 ....
8 ....
9 ....

4 PHYSICAL APPEARANCE

Look in a mirror, and write a description of yourself. Talk briefly about your
height, weight and build, and describe your face in detail.

....
....
....
....
....
....
....
....

5 STAR PICTURE

Look at the pictures of Sandy Wellings, who has just jumped to stardom as Cleopatra in the new London musical hit *Cleo*, and the other information about her.
Write a short magazine article, describing her appearance, and saying what she is like.

Date of birth: 8.9.64.
Father: Australian.
Mother: Italian.
Came to London: 1979.
Favourite colour: green.
Interests: music, horse-riding, walking, travel.
Favourite reading: romantic historical novels.
Home: London flat with three cats.
Travel: Australia, Middle East, Southern Europe.
Ambition: to own and run a recording studio.

....
....
....
....
....
....
....
....
....
....

Unit 3 Relating past events

1 PREVIOUS EVENTS

Complete the following sentences using the Past Perfect tense.

1 I apologised to him for all the inconvenience I *had caused.* ....

2 I took back to the library all the books I ....

3 I was thoroughly ashamed of the stupid mistake I ....

4 On the application form I had to list all the schools I ....

5 I couldn't decide whether to apply for the job I ....

6 He couldn't pay back the money I ....

7 I complained to the examiner about the mark I ....

8 I wanted to show her the presents I ....

9 I threw away the pieces of the vase I ....

2 CHANGES IN THE PAST

Develop these sentences into paragraphs. Explain what things *were* like
and what changes *had* taken place.

1 When I got home from my holiday I found that my parents had made all
  kinds of changes to our flat. *They had redecorated the sitting*
  room, and there were two new pictures on the walls. They'd
  moved the big wardrobe from their bedroom into mine, and
  in its place there was now a new dressing table.

  ....

  ....

  ....

2 It was more than five years since I had last seen my cousin. ....

  ....

  ....

  ....

  ....

⟫→

13

....

....

....

3 When I went back to the village where I had grown up, it was almost

unrecognisable. ....

....

....

....

....

....

3 PREVIOUS ACTIVITIES

Add three sentences about the following people, explaining what they had possibly been doing.

1 Jack's eyes were all red...

a) *He'd been peeling onions.*

b) *He'd been watching TV for ten hours.*

c) ....

2 Angela was out of breath...

a) ....

b) ....

c) ....

3 Peter was covered in dirt...

a) ....

b) ....

c) ....

4 Sheila felt very cold...

a) ....

b) ....

c) ....

5 Michael couldn't stand up straight...

a) ....

b) ....

c) ....

4   RELATIVE CLAUSES

Join the following sentences together using a non-defining relative clause.

1   Finally Brown (Willis had been sharing an office with him) decided to retire.
Finally Brown, with whom Willis had been sharing an office, decided to retire.

2   Mrs Aldrich (she was married with two children) never recovered consciousness.

3   The old house (the family had lived in it for 300 years) was finally sold.

4   Mary noticed that he was wearing her ring (she had lost it five years before).

5   Nobody liked the eldest son (old Lord Banbury had left all his money to him).

6   He proudly showed me round his house (he had paid £100,000 for it).

7   He became quite fond of Brixton Prison (he had spent so much of his life there).

8   Harold (she had always been in love with him) finally asked her to marry him).

9   Godfrey (his parents had been in the theatre) decided to become an actor himself.

>>>→

10 In 1948 (he was still a student then) he joined the Conservative Party.

....

....

5 FLASHBACKS IN NARRATION

Fill in the three gaps in the story below with suitable narrative.

Henrietta was confident as she walked into the interview room. She knew she
was the most experienced applicant for the job. She had ....

....

....

....

She was confident about the way she looked, too. ....

....

....

....

She sat down and looked up at the three members of the interview board. Her
mouth fell open as she recognised the tall blond man sitting opposite her. It was
Andrew. She had first met Andrew ....

....

....

....

....

Her memories were interrupted by a voice saying 'I believe you've done this
sort of work before, Miss Coombs'. She looked up and saw Andrew smiling at her
kindly. 'Excuse me,' she mumbled, and she stood up and rushed out of the room.

Unit 4   Attitudes and reactions

1   VERBS AND ADJECTIVES

Below are some remarks made by Colin which show his attitudes to certain things.
For each, describe his *general* attitude in three different ways.

1 'His clothes are so dirty! How disgusting!'

  a) *Colin is disgusted by people who wear dirty clothes.*

  b) *He finds*

  c) *People with dirty clothes*

2 'Oh no – not another cocktail party! What a bore!'

  a) ....

  b) ....

  c) ....

3 'She's got long blond hair – immensely attractive.'

  a) ....

  b) ....

  c) ....

4 'He's scratching himself again. How irritating!'

  a) ....

  b) ....

  c) ....

5 'Look how fast he's driving. I'm really impressed.'

  a) ....

  b) ....

  c) ....

2   IF THERE'S ONE THING...

What might Colin say in the situations below? Begin 'If there's one thing...'

1 Someone's singing in the bath. It's getting on Colin's nerves.
  If there's one thing that gets on my nerves, it's people who
  sing in the bath.

                ⟫→

2 Someone's laughing at Colin. It's infuriating him.

....

....

3 Someone's taken Colin's pen without asking. He's angry.

....

....

4 It's after midnight, and the people next door are playing loud music. Colin objects to it.

....

....

5 Someone's just spat in the street. Colin is offended.

....

....

6 Colin's just seen someone with purple and green hair. He can't stand this.

....

....

3 THE WAY

Write three sentences showing your attitude to each of the following, using
the way...

1 sports commentators

a) *I like the way sports commentators give you the players' background.* (like)

b) *One thing that annoys me about them is the way they shout too much.* (annoy)

c) *What I can't stand about them is the way*

.... (can't stand)

2 parents

a) *I*

.... (object to)

b) *One thing*

.... (appreciate)

c) *What*

.... (upset)

3 shopkeepers

a) ....
.... (dislike)

b) ....
.... (like)

c) ....
.... (irritate)

4 cats

a) ....
.... (love)

b) ....
.... (interest)

c) ....
.... (hate)

4 CHARACTER DEFINITIONS

What would you expect the following types of people to do? Write definitions.

1 A considerate person *is someone who is careful not to hurt your*
feelings. ....

2 An unreliable person ....
....

3 A stingy person ....
....

4 A thick-skinned person ....
....

5 A vain person ....
....

6 A sceptical person ....
....

7 An optimistic person ....
....

5 REACTIONS

Talk about your reactions to a film you saw recently. Use the list of questions below to help you.

In general did you find it exciting / boring / interesting / amusing?
What did you find particularly impressive / disappointing?
Was the story too simple / too complicated / convincing?
How good was the acting / the camerawork / the music?
Were the characters realistic?
Was it too short / too long?
Did you learn anything from it?
How did you feel at the end?

....

....

....

....

....

....

....

....

....

....

....

....

....

....

Unit 5   Duration

---

1   HOW LONG...?

Ask these people questions with **How long...?**. Write their answers using the words in brackets.

1   Tim telephoned his father this morning. (five minutes)

    You: *How long did you speak to him for?*

    Tim: *I spoke to him for about five minutes.*

2   Jane wrote an essay last night. (two hours)

    You: ....

    Jane: ....

3   Tony plays golf. (four years)

    You: ....

    Tony: ....

4   William doesn't play the guitar any more. (two years)

    You: ....

    William: ....

5   Cindy is going away on holiday tomorrow. (three weeks)

    You: ....

    Cindy: ....

6   Eleanor regularly flies to America. (seven hours)

    You: ....

    Eleanor: ....

7   Cyril slept well last night. (ten hours)

    You: ....

    Cyril: ....

8   Liza has a cold. (three days)

    You: ....

    Liza: ....

9   Mandy is going to drive to the coast this afternoon. (two hours)

    You: ....

    Mandy: ....

》》→

10 John doesn't live in England any more. (six months)

You: ....

John: ....

2 TIME EXPRESSIONS

Fill the gaps in the sentences below with **for, in, until** or **by**.

1 She studied medicine .... the age of 25.

2 They got the lunch ready .... 12.30.

3 He learnt to swim .... six weeks.

4 They lived in Newcastle .... 1973.

5 My father ran a bookshop .... two years.

6 We did all our housework .... a couple of hours.

7 We did some housework .... a couple of hours.

8 I finished my homework .... suppertime.

9 We discussed politics .... three in the morning.

10 They reached the top of the mountain .... four hours.

11 I borrowed my neighbour's power-drill .... a few days.

12 He got all the letters typed .... four o'clock.

13 The concert was over .... half past nine.

14 He saved up £200 .... Easter.

15 I studied French .... five years.

16 She became a qualified physiotherapist .... twelve months.

17 I dug the garden .... a couple of hours.

18 He stayed in bed .... lunchtime.

3 GETTING DELAYED

Continue the following in two ways:

a) using **didn't...for/till**
b) using **was...before...**

1 They were sure they would find the oasis in a few hours (six days)

   a) *but they didn't find it for six days.* ....

   b) *but it was six days before they found it.* ....

2 I was sure I'd finish the crossword in a few minutes (more than half an hour)

   a) *but* ....

   b) *but* ....

3 His parents expected him to marry young (48)

   a) ....

   b) ....

4 I meant to mow the lawn during the weekend (mid-week)

   a) ....

   b) ....

5 She thought she would go back home before long (several years)

   a) ....

   b) ....

6 Everyone expected the war to be over in a few days (almost a year)

   a) ....

   b) ....

4 IT DEPENDS

Write three sentences with **It depends** for each of the questions below. Use the ideas given.

1 How long does it take you to read a novel?

   a) The number of pages?
   b) How much time do you have?
   c) Is it enjoyable to read?

   a) *It depends on the number of pages.*

   b) *It depends on how much time you have.*

   c) *It depends on whether it is enjoyable to read or not.*

2 What time do you get up in the morning?

   a) How do you feel?
   b) Is it a weekday or the weekend?
   c) What time did you go to bed the night before?

   a) ....

   b) ....

   c) ....

3 How long does it take you to cook a meal?

    a)   The recipe?
    b)   Have you ever cooked it before?
    c)   How many people is it for?

    a) ....

    b) ....

    c) ....

4 Do you walk to work?

    a)   Is it raining or not?
    b)   The time of year?
    c)   How much time do you have?

    a) ....

    b) ....

    c) ....

5 Do you have to book for the theatre in advance?

    a)   How long has the play been on?
    b)   Is the play popular?
    c)   The night of the week?

    a) ....

    b) ....

    c) ....

5 PAST, PRESENT AND FUTURE

Christine is a journalist. Write a paragraph about Christine, using the information below, and giving the *duration* of each of the things she has done, is doing and is going to do, using **for**. Add any details you like.

Work for Times Newspapers (four years ago – now)
Study French at Cambridge University (1970–1973)
Travel round Europe (1973–1974)
Work for *Yorkshire Herald* (1974–1976)

Live in small flat (four years ago – now)
Look for bigger flat (three months ago – now)

Write children's books (three years ago – now)
Plan to take a break from journalism (next week – a few months later)
Go on holiday (next week – two weeks later)
Work on a new book (three weeks' time – two or three months later)

Christine is a journalist. She has been working for Times Newspapers
for four years now.

....

....

....

....

....

....

....

....

....

....

....

Revision crossword   Units 1–5

Across

1   Hair grown on the chin. (5)

4   He laughs at my jokes. He is .... by my jokes. (6)

8   The letter was from my brother, from .... I had recently borrowed some money. (4)

9   Next morning, the ground was wet. It had been .... during the night. (7)

10 He stood looking out of the window as .... he was waiting for someone. (6)

11 She has an .... face (= egg-shaped). (4)

12 Opposite of beautiful. (4)

14 He should see a doctor – he .... rather ill to me. (5)

17 I can't stand his accent. It really .... on my nerves. (4)

19 If there's 27 *across* thing that .... me cross, it's people who leave doors open. (5)

22 I thought the meeting would only last for a few minutes, but it was three hours .... we were able to leave. (6)

24 She's about 34 or 35. She's in her .... thirties. (6)

27 If there's .... thing that *19 across* me cross, it's people who leave doors open. (3)

28 This crossword comes after 5. (4)

29 They were exhausted. They .... the whole day working in the garden. (3,5)

31 I've been working here .... August last year. (5)

33 It usually .... her about half an hour to get to work. (5)

35 This is my first .... to London. (5)

38 Have you .... been attacked by muggers? (4)

40 No, but I've .... my car stolen. (3)

42 His hair isn't straight. It's ....y. (4)

43 If there's *27 across* thing that annoys me, ...'... having to sit in traffic jams. (3)

45 I can't remember whether he was born in 1957 or 1958 – some time in the .... fifties, anyway. (4)

46 I .... astrology rather fascinating. (4)

48 Mrs Thomas, ... daughter works in the chemist's, has been taken ill. (5)

49 We couldn't get a ticket – they had all .... sold. (4)

50 That's the first time I've .... a mile in less than five minutes. (3)

51 It took us all .... to repair the damage. It was morning by the time we had finished. (5)

Down

1 I didn't find the programme very interesting. In fact, I thought it was rather .... (6)

2 What've you been doing? You look .... you've been up all night. (2,2)

3 It's all right. I'm quite used to .... my own washing up. (5)

4 Cross, very annoyed. (5)

5 It was a long journey. We didn't arrive .... nine o'clock. (5)

6 Have you ever .... British beer? (5)

7 Their lights are out. They seem .... gone out. (2,4)

8 I play tennis with Kate, ... lives just across the road. (3)

12 I can't go to sleep now. I'm not .... to going to bed as early as this. (4)

13 Caviar tastes .... jam with fish in it. (4)

15 Mr Wilkinson fell .... the stretcher and broke his leg. (3)

16 Put that awful cigar out, please. It .... terrible. (6)

18 He leant against the wall, as if he was .... faint. (5,2)

20 She's an old friend. I've .... her for more than ten years. (5)

21 I had only met him a few times, but he .... very pleasant. (6)

23 'How long does it take to drive to your place?' 'That depends .... traffic.' (2,3)

25 I .... all the housework by lunchtime, and then I went out. (3)

26 Part of the mouth. (3)

29 I .... lived in five different countries, including this one. (4)

30 'Why do you keep falling over?' 'I've never been .... ing before.' (3)

32 This is the first time ...'...... *39 down* a horse. It's fun. (3)

34 You're .... – you only think of yourself. (7)

36 See *42 down*.

37 I like .... he always says 'Good morning'. (3,3)

39 This is the first time *32 down* .... a horse. It's fun. (6)

41 I once .... my old car all the way to Athens. (5)

42 and 36 He doesn't have a *1 across*. He's ....-........... (5–6)

44 You .... as if you've got a cold. (5)

47 He worked as a salesman .... a couple of years. (3)

Unit 6   Reporting

1   REPORTED SPEECH

Report the following remarks, beginning **He told me...**

1   My father's ill.
He told me his father was ill.

2   I'll tell her when I see her.

....

....

3   I've been sleeping very badly.

....

4   If they're waiting for you, you ought to go.

....

....

5   The price of petrol's going to go up.

....

....

6   I'm sure she won't mind if you use the phone.

....

....

7   I wasn't invited to the wedding.

....

....

8   I've had my car serviced.

....

9   I'm reading that book you lent me.

....

....

10 They don't play as much tennis as they used to.

....

....

11 Since they've already got one, there's no point in giving them one.

....

....

12 You look as if you haven't eaten for weeks.

....

....

2 SURPRISE SURPRISE

Respond with surprise to each of the following, in three different ways. Use these expressions in your answers:

told me / said... thought...
didn't tell me... didn't realise / know...

1 I've been reading a book of Spanish poetry.
   a) *Really? I didn't know you liked poetry.*
   b) *What? But you told me last week you'd forgotten all your Spanish.*
   c) *But I thought you were reading those Italian plays.*

2 I'm afraid I can't afford to come to the concert.
   a) ....
   b) ....
   c) ....
   ....

3 My two daughters are coming to stay with me during the holidays.
   a) ....
   b) ....
   c) ....
   ....

4 Don't get too friendly with George – he's an awful bore.
   a) ....
   b) ....
   c) ....
   ....

5 Come round to dinner tonight – I'm cooking an enormous meal.

a) ....

b) ....

c) ....

....

3 REPORTING VERBS: FACTS

Report each conversation below in two sentences, using the verbs in brackets.

1 Smith: It was you who stole the car, wasn't it?
   Brown: Nonsense. Of course I didn't.

a) *Smith accused Brown of* .... (accuse)

b) .... (deny)

2 Smith: But your fingerprints were found all over it.
   Brown: I'm innocent, I tell you! Innocent!

a) ....
   .... (point out)

b) .... (insist)

3 Brown: The owner lent it to me.
   Smith: If you keep on lying, you'll be in trouble.

a) .... (claim)

b) ....
   .... (warn)

4 Brown: Well, all right, I took the car.
   Smith: Look, if you tell us what happened, you won't be prosecuted.
   Brown: I had to take it, because someone was following me and I used it to escape in.

a) .... (admit)

b) ....
   .... (assure)

c) ....
   .... (explain)

4 REPORTING VERBS: INFLUENCING AND TAKING ACTION

Choose one of the verbs in the list to report each of the remarks below.

promise	advise	suggest	urge
threaten	recommend	insist	beg

1 I can't tell you how important it is for you to give up smoking.
   He urged me to give up smoking.
   ....

2 You've got to lend me the money! Oh, please, please!
   ....

3 Why don't you paint the ceiling yellow?
   ....

4 I'll buy you an ice cream if you're good.
   ....
   ....

5 You should spend a week in Scotland – it's lovely.
   ....
   ....

6 No, I've already told you – *I'm* going to pay.
   ....

7 You really ought to have your roof repaired, you know.
   ....

8 I'll report you to the police if you don't do what I say.
   ....
   ....

5 REPORTING A CONVERSATION

Write a report of the conversation below, using where appropriate the verbs you have learnt in the unit.

Salesman:	This is a lovely pair of jeans, sir. They're a new style – they've just come in from America.
You:	No thank you.
Salesman:	I think you're making a mistake, sir. They're the best jeans you'll find anywhere.
You:	But they're not even new. Look – the colour's all been washed out...
Salesman:	Of course they're new, sir. It's the latest fashion to wear them that colour.
You:	And they've got patches on them. They've been used!
Salesman:	Well, yes, that's true, they have got a couple of little patches on them, haven't they? But they're still a bargain. Come on, sir, why don't you try them on and see how they look?
You:	What, at £25 a pair? No thank you!

I was in a clothes shop the other day and the

salesman tried to persuade me

....

....

....

....

....

....

....

....

....

....

....

....

....

....

....

Unit 7   Deductions and explanations

1   MUST, MIGHT / MAY & CAN'T

Rewrite the sentences below, using **must**, **can't** or **might / may**.

1   I'm sure they've arrived.
They must have arrived.
....

2   I'm sure she's not having lunch.

....

3   Perhaps he didn't hear you.

....

4   I'm sure it hasn't been snowing.

....

5   Perhaps he wasn't telling the truth.

....

6   I'm sure you're exhausted.

....

7   Maybe he was delayed.

....

8   I'm convinced you haven't forgotten my name.

....

9   I'm sure I was dreaming.

....

10 I'm sure you're imagining things.

....

11 It's possible that they're going away.

....

12 I'm sure they weren't serious.

....

13 Obviously he's been kidnapped.

....

⟫→

14 Perhaps she's going to ring.

....

15 I'm sure they weren't informed.

....

2 CONCLUSIONS FROM EVIDENCE

Draw three different conclusions from each of the following pieces of evidence.

1 There are five bottles of milk on their front door step.

a) *They must have forgotten to cancel their milk deliveries before they went away.*

b) *They can't have woken up yet.*

c) *There must be some guests staying with them.*

2 There are two large suitcases in her car.

a) ....

b) ....

c) ....

....

3 I saw the Wheelers coming out of the American Embassy this morning.

a) ....

b) ....

c) ....

....

4 His name isn't in the phone book.

a) ....

b) ....

c) ....

....

5 Her coat's on the floor.

a) ....

b) ....

c) ....

....

3 GIVING REASONS FOR DEDUCTIONS

Explain the following deductions using an **If....** sentence.

1 He can't be a soldier – he's not wearing a uniform.
   If he was a soldier, he would be wearing a uniform.

2 There can't be anyone at home – the car's gone.

   ....

   ....

3 They must be having an argument – they've shut the door.

   ....

   ....

4 She can't have been enjoying herself – she left early.

   ....

   ....

5 He must have been here recently – the kettle's warm.

   ....

   ....

6 He can't be working at the library – I haven't seen him there.

   ....

   ....

7 She must know English – she was listening to the BBC.

   ....

   ....

8 They must have got lost – they're not here yet.

   ....

   ....

4 DEDUCTIONS AND REASONS

John is a liar. In column 1 below are some claims that he made, and in column
2 the evidence that shows he was lying. Match the claims to the pieces of evidence,
and write for each one:
(a) a deduction with **must** or **can't**
(b) a supporting reason with **If...**

Claims	*Evidence*
I haven't been out today.	He was trembling.
I wrote that essay myself.	He doesn't have a stamp in his passport.
I've never been arrested.	He wasn't picked for the school team.
I went to the US last summer.	His photo's in police files.
I went to school yesterday.	He's got an Edinburgh accent.
I don't smoke.	It's in someone else's handwriting.
I wasn't frightened.	His coat's wet.
I'm a fantastic football player.	No one saw him there.
I've never lived in Scotland.	His clothes smell of tobacco.

1 *He must have been out today. If he hadn't been out, his coat*
  wouldn't be wet.

2 ....

3 ....

4 ....

5 ....

6 ....

7 ....

8 ....

9 ....

5 EXPLANATIONS

Example The number of people going to cinemas is still going down...

> This doesn't necessarily mean that people are not watching as many films as they used to. More films are being shown on TV these days, and a large number of video recorders are being sold. This suggests that many people prefer to watch films at home rather than go to the cinema.

In the same way, say what each of the following **suggests** / **means** / **indicates** (or **doesn't suggest** / **mean** / **indicate**). Write two or three sentences about each.

1 Fewer people are learning foreign languages at language schools these days...

....

....

....

....

....

2 There has been a large increase in the number of magazines concerned with home computers...

....

....

....

....

....

3 Recent figures show that only about 10% of schoolchildren have ever stepped inside a bookshop...

....

....

....

....

....

Unit 8 Advantages and disadvantages

1 'EFFECT' VERBS

Rewrite the sentences about supermarkets below, beginning with the words given.
Use an appropriate verb from the list for each answer.

encourage   enable   allow   **make it easier**
discourage   save   force   **make it more difficult**

1 People tend to buy more in supermarkets because of the open display.

   The open display *encourages people to buy more*.

2 People can also steal things more easily because of the open display.

   The open display ....

   ....

3 There's a wide range of goods, so you can do all your shopping in one place.

   The wide range of goods ....

   ....

4 Some supermarkets use cameras, so that people are less likely to steal things.

   The use of cameras ....

   ....

5 Most supermarkets have a car park next door, so customers don't have to carry
   their shopping a long way.

   Having a car park next door ....

   ....

6 Supermarkets buy in bulk, so they can sell things at cut prices.

   Buying in bulk ....

   ....

7 Because supermarkets sell things at cut prices, smaller shops have to lower their
   prices too.

   The cut prices in supermarkets ....

   ....

8 Because of the competition from supermarkets, it's harder for smaller shops to stay
   in business.

   The competition from supermarkets ....

   ....

38

2 ADVANTAGES AND DISADVANTAGES

Write a paragraph about the advantages and disadvantages of shopping in super-markets rather than in small shops. Use some of the ideas in exercise 1 if you wish, and use some of the following expressions:

advantage	good thing	trouble
disadvantage	bad thing	drawback

....

....

....

....

....

....

....

....

....

....

....

....

3 POSITIVE AND NEGATIVE ADVICE

Complete the following sentences with: (a) **there's no point / it's not worth**
(b) **might as well.**

1 Since they don't appreciate good food anyway...

  a) *there's no point in cooking them anything special.*

  b) *you might as well heat up something out of a tin.*

2 If the theatre never fills up anyway...

  a) ....

  b) ....

3 Since you're only going to read the book once...

  a) ....

  b) ....

4 If they're going to televise the match live...

  a) ....

  b) ....

⟫⟫→

5 Since everyone else will be wearing jeans...

    a) ....

    b) ....

6 If you're sure the police will find you anyway...

    a) ....

    b) ....

4 FUTURE POSSIBILITIES

A friend of yours is thinking of visiting Britain (or another country), but can't decide:

1 whether to go by car or by train
2 whether to stay in hotels / guest houses or stay with friends
3 whether to go in winter or summer

Tell him what would happen if he did each of these things.

1 car or train? *If you went by car you wouldn't have to carry your luggage, and you'd be free to travel anywhere. If there were several of you, you'd also save money on fares, but you'd be in trouble if you had an accident. If you went by train*

....

....

....

....

2 hotel or friends? ....

....

....

....

....

....

....

3 winter or summer? ....

....

....

....

....

....

....

....

5 TELEPHONES

Write three paragraphs about the advantages and disadvantages of having a
telephone. The first paragraph should be about the advantages, the second about
the disadvantages and the third a conclusion. Use the ideas below to help you, and
any others that you think of.

people wake you up	TV programmes interrupted
you can get an alarm call	wrong numbers
easy to get in touch with people	useful in an emergency
expense	you don't know who's ringing until you
friends use it without paying	answer

....

....

....

....

....

....

....

....

....

....

....

....

....

....

....

....

Unit 9 Clarifying

---

1 INFORMATION QUESTIONS

Fill the gaps below with information questions.

1 A: *What was the weather like?*

   B: It was cold and rather windy.

2 A: ....

   B: I take 36, actually. I've got rather small feet.

3 A: ....

   B: Ooh, after every meal, usually.

4 A: ....

   B: I've got a Labrador.

5 A: ....

   B: I'm going to have it shampooed and set.

6 A: Mr Coombs left £20,000 when he died.

   B: Really? ....

7 A: I only took one photo while I was in Rome.

   B: Did you? ....

8 A: Ow! I think I've been stung.

   B: ....

9 A: I've managed to borrow that £100 I need.

   B: ....

10 A: I had a really strange dream last night.

   B: ....

11 A: Sh! I'm listening to the Prime Minister on the radio.

   B: ....

2 INDIRECT QUESTIONS

Combine the following pairs of sentences into indirect questions.

1 What does he do for a living? I often wonder.
   I often wonder what he does for a living.

2 Does she like classical music? Can you remember?
   Can you remember whether
   ....

3 Where are you going for your holidays? Have you decided yet?
   ....
   ....

4 Are you coming tomorrow? I need to know now.
   ....
   ....

5 Did you ever find your camera? I've been meaning to ask you.
   ....
   ....

6 What crime has he been charged with? Do you know?
   ....
   ....

7 What time does the concert start? I've no idea.
   ....
   ....

8 Did he look angry? Did you notice?
   ....
   ....

9 What is your brother's name? I've forgotten.
   ....
   ....

3 CHECKING UP

Ask questions beginning **Is / Was it...?**, as in the examples.

1 Excuse me, sir. Did you order three steaks or four?
   Excuse me, sir. Was it three or four steaks that you ordered?

2 Has your father been helping you with your homework? Or has your mother?
   Is it your father or your mother who's been helping you with your homework?

3 Do remind me – did we last meet in Paris or Madrid?
   Do remind me–was it ....

   ....

4 I've completely forgotten – do we have to come early tomorrow or the day after?

   ....

   ....

5 He's engaged to a Japanese girl, I think. Or maybe she's Chinese.

   ....

   ....

6 Do you grow flowers or vegetables in your garden?

   ....

   ....

7 Did you want to speak to the manager or the assistant manager?

   ....

   ....

8 I can't remember – are you going to London by bus or by train?

   ....

   ....

9 John's father owns a garage, doesn't he? Or am I thinking of Tony?

   ....

   ....

10 Can you remind me – are the Spencers arriving on Saturday or Sunday?

   ....

   ....

4 CORRECTING

Correct the statements below.

1 Charles Dickens was born in Stratford-on-Avon.
   It wasn't Charles Dickens who was born in Stratford-on-Avon. It
   was Shakespeare.

2 Doctors look after your teeth.
   It isn't doctors

3 Marco Polo discovered America.

4 The sun causes the tides.

5 Democracy started in Italy.

6 Agatha Christie wrote the James Bond stories.

7 India has the largest population in the world.

8 Martin Luther King was assassinated in Dallas.

5 REPORTED QUESTIONS

A well-known singer arrived in England last week. At the airport she was asked
a lot of questions by reporters. Report the questions, using **asked her** or **wanted to
know**.

1 'How long are you staying?'
   They wanted to know how long she was staying.

2 'Are you planning to give any concerts while you're here?'
   They asked her

3 'Have you written any new songs recently?'

4 'When is your next record going to be released?'

5 'What have you been doing since your last visit?'

6 'Are you glad you're here?'

7 'Do you think your next record will be a hit?'

8 'Why didn't your husband come with you?'

9 'Will you be staying in London?'

Unit 10   Wishes and regrets

---

1   WISHES

Imagine you are in the situations below. Write three wishes for each: (a) with **would**
(b) with **could** (c) with the Past tense.

1 You're in bed with flu.

   a) *If only my temperature would go down.*

   b) *I wish I could get up.*

   c) *I wish there wasn't so much traffic outside.*

2 You're lost.

   a) ....

   b) ....

   c) ....

3 You're out of work.

   a) ....

   b) ....

   c) ....

4 You're trying to communicate with a foreigner who doesn't speak your language.

   a) ....

   b) ....

   c) ....

5 You're in love.

   a) ....

   b) ....

   c) ....

2 EXPLAINING WISHES: 'IF...' SENTENCES

Choose any *two* of your wishes for each situation above, and explain them using
If...

1 a) *If my temperature went down, I wouldn't have to stay in bed.*

   b) *If there wasn't so much traffic outside, I'd be able to get some*
      sleep.

2 a) ....
      ....

   b) ....
      ....

3 a) ....
      ....

   b) ....
      ....

4 a) ....
      ....

   b) ....
      ....

5 a) ....
      ....

   b) ....
      ....

3 FANTASISING

Write short paragraphs beginning as follows:

1 If I could have any job I wanted, *I would* ....
....
....
....
....

2 If I had six months' paid holiday, ...
....
....
....
....

3 If I only had three months to live, ...
....
....
....
....

4 If I was the Minister of Education, ...
....
....
....
....

4 REGRETS

Regret doing the things below. Add an **If...** sentence showing the consequence of your action, and a **Then...** sentence, showing a further consequence.

1 You went to a party.
   I wish I hadn't gone to that party. If I hadn't gone, I wouldn't have got drunk. And then I wouldn't have had that accident on the way home.

2 You forgot your wedding anniversary.

   ....

   ....

   ....

   ....

3 You didn't check the oil in your car.

   ....

   ....

   ....

   ....

4 You won the football pools.

   ....

   ....

   ....

   ....

5 You didn't set your alarm clock.

   ....

   ....

   ....

   ....

6 You lost your passport.

   ....

   ....

   ....

   ....

7 You didn't unplug your television.

....

....

....

....

5   COULD HAVE AND NEEDN'T HAVE

Add two sentences to the remarks below: (a) with **could have** (b) with **needn't have**.

1 You didn't tell me you could do electrical repairs.
   a) *You could have mended my radio for me.*
   b) *I needn't have taken my radio to the shop to be repaired.*

2 I wish I'd known their telephone had been repaired.
   a) ....
   b) ....

3 If only you'd told me you were ill.
   a) ....
   b) ....

4 I didn't realise I still had £10 in my pocket.
   a) ....
   b) ....

5 I didn't know I was going to win all that money.
   a) ....
   b) ....

6 I had no idea it would be so warm here.
   a) ....
   b) ....

Revision crossword Units 6–10

Across

1 The main .... of being unemployed is that there's no money coming in. (12)

6 He ....'... have gone swimming. He hasn't taken his swimming things with him. (4)

10 I'm not sure .... Yellowstone Park is in Canada or the USA. (7)

12 He asked us what .... carrying in our suitcases. (2,4)

14 Congratulations. I didn't know you were .... to get married. (5)

15 The film was so boring that we left before the .... (3)

17 'What crime was he charged with?' 'With .... – he attacked one of his neighbours.' (7)

20 By sea? But I thought you .... all your letters by airmail. (4)

21 If you had better qualifications, ... find it easier to get a good job. (3,5)

22 ... . they would turn that music down. Then I could concentrate on my work. (1,4)

27 What .... having for dinner? Something nice, I hope. (3,2)

28 There are a lot of .... in these clues. (4)

30 Paul finds it strange driving in England. He .... to driving on the right. (2,4)

31 They assured me .... everything would be all right. (4)

33 It's not .... going to the park now. It's almost dark. (5)

35 She insisted that she .... them several letters, but that they hadn't replied. (3,7)

37 The money's gone! Someone .... have stolen it! (4)

39 Season tickets .... people to travel without having to queue up to buy a ticket every time. (5)

41 More and more robots are being used in factories. That .... that unemployment is going to continue to rise. (5)

42 One advantage of living in a big .... is that there are lots of places to go in the evenings. (4)

43 I was half-way down the road when I remembered that I ....'... turned off the central heating. (5)

44 I recommended .... see a doctor, but he didn't take any notice. (3,2)

46 What a pity you didn't tell me you would be late. I ....'... have got up so early. (6)

47 How would you like your .... ? Rare? Medium? Well done? (5)

48 He was 70 a couple of years ago, I think. Anyway, he's somewhere in his .... seventies. (5)

Down

1 She told me that she .... the crossword every morning on the train. (3)

2 Dishwashers .... you having to wash up by hand. (4)

3 What have you .... with my book? I can't find it anywhere. (4)

4 There's nothing else to do. I suppose we might .... watch the film on TV. (2,4)

5 ....'s no point in waiting for that shop to open. They close early on Wednesdays. (5)

7 My doctor .... me to give up smoking, so I did. (7)

8 He told me he was a teacher. He said he .... English in a language school. (6)

9 Recommend strongly. (4)

11 I didn't believe him when he said he always .... his money under his mattress. But I looked, and it was there. (3)

12 When the policeman found me sitting outside my front door in my pyjamas, he wanted to know .... was doing there. (4,1)

13 Has he come back? I thought he .... still in France. (3)

16 It's .... crying about it. There's nothing you can do. (2,3)

18 What .... of television have you got – colour or black and white? (4)

19 She denied stealing the coat, and claimed she had .... it in a department store. (6)

20 If the bed hadn't been so uncomfortable, I would have .... much better. (5)

23 They .... arrived by now if they'd caught the early train. (5,4)

24 I explained that I .... already had my breakfast. (3)

25 When he claimed they were new, I pointed .... that the jeans had some holes in them. (3)

26 The trouble .... dishwashers is that they're so expensive to run. (4)

29 What a fool I was to hit that car. I ....'...... been driving more carefully. (8)

32 If I'd decided to use the stairs, I would never have got .... in the lift. (5)

33 It's often wet in England (and it sounds like *10 across*!). (7)

34 If .... had used the stairs instead of the lift. (4,1)

36 The Minister admitted that the unemployment figures were still .... but promised that things would begin to improve soon. (6)

38 The new law only encouraged people .... the drug. (2,4)

40 '.......... guitar is that?' 'It's my sister's.' (5)

41 How .... people are coming to the party? (4)

45 'Where's the car key?' 'I'm not sure. It .... be in the desk.' (3)

Unit 11 Events in sequence

1 WHEN AND AS SOON AS

Continue the following half-sentences in a suitable way.

1 a) When I broke the vase   *I burst into tears.*
   b) When I'd broken the vase   *I picked up the pieces and threw them away.*

2 a) When I made the bed   ....
   ....

   b) When I'd made the bed   ....
   ....

3 a) As soon as the Prime Minister resigned   ....
   ....

   b) As soon as the Prime Minister had resigned   ....
   ....

4 a) When he knocked me down   ....
   ....

   b) When he had knocked me down   ....
   ....

5 a) As soon as the thief opened the window   ....
   ....

   b) As soon as the thief had opened the window   ....
   ....

6 a) When the police searched the car   ....
   ....

   b) When the police had searched the car   ....
   ....

7 a) As soon as the teacher went into the classroom   ....
   ....

   b) As soon as the teacher had gone into the classroom   ....
   ....

2 THE RIGHT ORDER

Write two sentences for each pair of events below, showing that the person did them in the right order.

1 read the instructions / switch on the machine

 a) Very sensibly, *he read the instructions before he switched on the machine.*

 b) Very sensibly, *he didn't switch on the machine until he'd read the instructions.*

2 measure the room / order the carpet

 a) Very wisely, ...

 ....

 b) Very wisely, ...

 ....

3 check his answers / leave the exam room

 a) Sensibly, ...

 ....

 b) Sensibly, ...

 ....

4 have their house decorated / put it up for sale

 a) Wisely, ...

 ....

 b) Wisely, ...

 ....

5 turn off the electric blanket / get into bed

 a) Sensibly, ...

 ....

 b) Sensibly, ...

 ....

3 THE WRONG ORDER

Imagine the people in exercise 2 above did things in the wrong order. Write two sentences for each, showing what they did wrong.

1 a) Stupidly, *he didn't read the instructions before he switched on the machine.*

  b) Stupidly, *he switched on the machine before he'd read the instructions.*

2 a) Foolishly, ...

  ....

  b) Foolishly, ...

  ....

3 a) Very unwisely, ...

  ....

  b) Very unwisely, ...

  ....

4 a) Rather unwisely, ...

  ....

  b) Rather unwisely, ...

  ....

5 a) Very stupidly, ...

  ....

  b) Very stupidly, ...

  ....

4 EVENTS IN RAPID SUCCESSION

Write two sentences showing how the following pairs of events happened in rapid succession: (a) using **only just** (b) using **No sooner**.

1 My grandfather retired / he had a heart attack
  a) *My grandfather had only just retired when he had a heart attack.*
  b) *No sooner had my grandfather retired than he had a heart attack.*

2 The Wilkinsons went to bed / Mrs Wilkinson heard a strange noise

    a) ....

        ....

    b) ....

        ....

3 The plane took off / three hijackers walked into the cabin

    a) ....

        ....

    b) ....

        ....

4 I sat down to watch my favourite programme / some friends turned up

    a) ....

        ....

    b) ....

        ....

5 The new exhibition hall was opened / it was destroyed by fire

    a) ....

        ....

    b) ....

        ....

6 We had the washing machine repaired / it broke down again

    a) ....

        ....

    b) ....

        ....

7 They got back from their honeymoon / they had a terrible quarrel

    a) ....

        ....

    b) ....

        ....

5 TELLING A STORY

Look at the pictures below, and tell the story.

An extraordinary thing happened when I came home from work the other day. I was walking up the path and had only just taken out my key when I noticed

....

....

....

....

....

....

....

....

....

....

....

....

Unit 12 Comparison

1 LARGE AND SMALL DIFFERENCES

Write comparative sentences based on the information below. In each case, write
two sentences: (a) with **than** (b) with **as...as...**

1 Car sales last year in Britain: British cars: 38%   foreign cars: 62%.

  a) *Foreign cars are a lot more popular than British cars.* .... (a lot)

  b) *British cars aren't nearly as popular as foreign cars.* .... (not nearly)

2 Exam marks: Jane: 75%   Paul: 42%.

  a) .... (far)

  b) .... (not nearly)

3 My house: £40,000.   Your house: £38,500.

  a) .... (slightly)

  b) .... (almost)

4 Dover–London: 117 km.   Harwich–London: 114 km.

  a) ....

      .... (a little)

  b) ....

      .... (not quite)

5 Yesterday's temperatures: Amsterdam: 19°   Beirut: 30°.

  a) ....

      .... (considerably)

  b) ....

      .... (not nearly)

6 Leeds: played 24 matches, won 17.   West Ham: played 24 matches, won 19.

  a) ....

      .... (slightly)

  b) ....

      .... (nearly)

7 Jane is 16½.   Paul is 17.

  a) .... (a bit)

  b) .... (not quite)

60

8 Maths exam: 70% failed.   History exam: 24% failed.

  a) *The maths exam was* ....

      .... (much)

  b) ....

      .... (not nearly)

2 NUMERICAL DIFFERENCES

Write sentences making numerical comparisons based on the information below.

1 George Hotel: Single room £12.50 per night
                Double room £21.50 per night

A double room at the George Hotel costs almost twice as much as a single room.

2 Estimated values: Cezanne, *Landscape in Provence*: £375,000
                Rembrandt, *Portrait of a merchant*: £125,000

The Cezanne is worth ....

3 Journey times Dover–Boulogne: Car ferry: 1½ hours
                       Hovercraft: 30 minutes

4 Long-distance telephone calls, cost per minute: Standard rate: 20 p
      Cheap rate (evenings and weekends): 5p

5 London–Glasgow: British Rail: 5 hours £46 return
           British Airways: 1 hour £90 return

  a) ....
  b) ....

6 British annual cinema attendances per person: 1950: 42
                1974: 14

  a) ....
  b) ....

7 Number of TV sets owned in Britain (1974): Colour: 5,600,000
                                                Black and white: 11,200,000

    ....

    ....

8 Americans killed since 1900: War: 400,000
                                  Road accidents: 2,000,000

    ....

    ....

3 COMPARISONS INVOLVING VERBS

Express the meanings of the sentences below with another comparative sentence,
beginning with the words given.

1 Those children ought to go to bed much earlier than they do.

   Those children go to bed *much later than they ought to.*......................

2 He's not supposed to drink quite as much as he does.

   He drinks ....

3 We hadn't expected them to arrive as early as they did.

   They arrived ....

4 I've never been as frightened as I was during that flight.

   During that flight, I ....

   ....

5 I had thought the room would be more expensive than it actually was.

   The room was actually ....

   ....

6 There are more foreign tourists this year than there have ever been before.

   There have never ....

   ....

7 You didn't need to get up nearly as early as you did.

   You got up ....

8 I would have liked to stay longer than I was able to.

   Unfortunately, I couldn't ....

   ....

9 It was quite unnecessary for you to tell them as much as you did.

   You told ....

   ....

4 HOLIDAYS

Last year you went to a crowded tourist resort for a holiday, and this year, for a change, you went on a camping holiday in the mountains. Look at the photos below, and compare the two places, and the holidays that you had there. Write about 150 words.

....

....

....

....

....

....

....

....

....

....

....

....

....

....

....

Unit 13   Processes

1   GETTING THE ORDER RIGHT

Write three sentences for each pair of actions below:
a) with **should...before...**
b) with **shouldn't...until...**
c) with **Otherwise...**

1   wash your hands / eat

  a) *You should wash your hands before you eat.*

  b) *You shouldn't eat until you've washed your hands.*

  c) *Otherwise you might get an infection.*

2   close your windows / go out

  a) ....

     ....

  b) ....

     ....

  c) ....

3   have some driving lessons / take your driving test

  a) ....

     ....

  b) ....

     ....

  c) ....

4   clean your teeth / go to bed

  a) ....

     ....

  b) ....

     ....

  c) ....

5 test the temperature of the water / bath the baby

   a) ....
....

   b) ....
....

   c) ....

2 GIVING INSTRUCTIONS

Look at the notes you took in 13.3 (Student's Book), and write full instructions for making Turkish coffee for four.

You put four cups of cold water ....

....

....

....

....

....

....

....

....

....

....

....

....

....

....

....

....

3   THE PASSIVE IN DESCRIBING PROCESSES

Look at the pictures and notes below, which show how instant coffee is produced,
and write a brief description of the process, using the Passive.

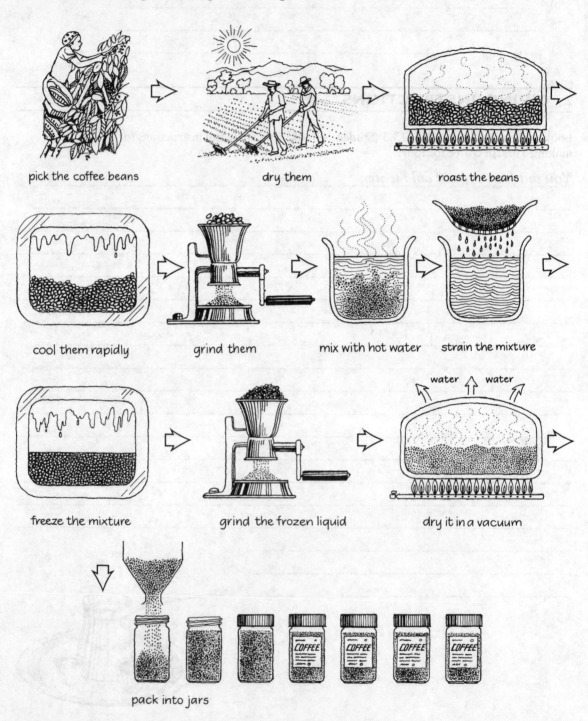

pick the coffee beans   dry them   roast the beans

cool them rapidly   grind them   mix with hot water   strain the mixture

freeze the mixture   grind the frozen liquid   dry it in a vacuum

water   water

pack into jars

The coffee beans are picked by hand. When this has been done, they
are laid in the open and dried by the sun. Then

....

....

....

....

....

....

4 NATURAL PROCESSES

Look at the diagram below, and explain what happens to water after it evaporates
in the sun.

When water evaporates in the sun

....

....

....

....

....

....

5 THE EDUCATIONAL PROCESS

Explain the educational process in your country, from the beginning of school to the
end of university. Include information about: ages, types of school, what the student
does at each stage, and examinations.

....

....

....

....

....

....

....

....

....

....

....

....

....

....

....

....

....

....

....

....

....

....

Unit 14 Prediction

---

1 PROBABILITIES

Answer the questions below according to the table, using **bound, certain, sure, likely, could, unlikely** and **definitely won't**.

		Yes		Maybe		No
1	Will it rain tomorrow?	×				
2	Will Milan win the Cup?				×	
3	Will there be much traffic?					×
4	Will they be at home?	×				
5	Will the letter arrive this week?			×		
6	Will rail fares go up again soon?		×			
7	Will there be plenty of food there?	×				
8	Will there be any tickets left?				×	
9	Will a cure be found for cancer?		×			
10	Will there be fewer tourists this year?	×				

1 *It's sure to rain tomorrow.* ....

2 ....

3 ....

4 ....

5 ....

6 ....

7 ....

8 ....

9 ....

10 ....

2 GIVING ADVICE WITH PREDICTIONS

Give two pieces of advice (one positive and one negative) in response to the remarks below. In each case make a prediction to explain your advice.

1 Do you think I should learn Chinese?
   a) *Yes, you should – it's sure to help you get a job.*
   b) *I wouldn't – you're unlikely to use it very much.*

2 I was thinking of building a swimming pool in the garden.
   a) ....
   ....
   b) ....
   ....

3 Perhaps I should take a week off work.
   a) ....
   ....
   b) ....
   ....

4 I can't decide whether to buy a house or not.
   a) ....
   ....
   b) ....
   ....

5 They've sent me the wrong size. Shall I write and complain?
   a) ....
   ....
   b) ....
   ....

6 I think I'll take the car when I go up to London.
   a) ....
   ....
   b) ....
   ....

3   OPTIMISTIC AND PESSIMISTIC PREDICTIONS

For each of the questions below write (a) an optimistic prediction and (b) a
pessimistic prediction. Use the ideas in brackets or ideas of your own. Use:
As long as   if   provided (that)   unless

1   Will he win the championship? (bad temper?)

a)   *Provided he doesn't lose his temper, there's a good chance that*
     he'll win the championship.

b)   *Unless he can control his bad temper, he's unlikely to win the*
     championship.

2   Will the murderer be caught? (witnesses?)

a)   ....

     ....

b)   ....

     ....

3   Will she get to university? (exam results?)

a)   ....

     ....

b)   ....

     ....

4   Will the party be a success? (how many people?)

a)   ....

     ....

b)   ....

     ....

5   Will the company survive? (strikes?)

a)   ....

     ....

b)   ....

     ....

6   Will they find a cure for cancer? (money for research?)

a)   ....

     ....

b)   ....

     ....

4 FUTURE DEVELOPMENTS

Write paragraphs predicting future developments concerning the topics below. Use some or all of the ideas given to help you.

1 *Energy*
Oil running out; prices; oilfield wars; other forms of energy; government control.

Oil is bound to run out in the next thirty years. Prices are likely to continue to rise quite rapidly, and unless new sources of energy are developed, governments may have to control the amount of oil that people are allowed to use. It is quite likely that wars will even be fought to get control of the oilfields. Nuclear power is certain to be used more widely in the future.

2 *World population*
Birth control; government control; starvation; new sources of food; disease.

....

....

....

....

....

....

3 *Technology*
Microchips; video-telephones, etc; transport; robots; unemployment.

....

....

....

....

....

....

4 *Space*
Cities in space; tourism in space; visiting other planets; war in space.

....

....

....

....

....

....

5 SUGGESTIONS AND EFFECTS

Now suggest solutions to the problems you wrote about in exercise 4. Say what we should do in each case and what effect the action would have.

1 *We should quickly develop other sources of energy such as solar power and wind power. Then we wouldn't use so much oil and oil supplies would last longer. The price of oil would probably go down too.*

2 ....

....

....

....

3 ....

....

....

....

4 ....

....

....

....

Unit 15 News

1 NEWS STORIES

From the notes below, write three news stories. Talk about what has happened, the
details of what happened, what has been happening, and the present situation.

1 Riots in east London; police arrest youth; group stone police; cars on fire;
windows smashed; police reinforcements; 60 injured, now in hospital; 43
arrested; now calm.

There have been serious riots in east London. The trouble began
earlier tonight when police arrested a youth who had broken a
window. A large group gathered and

....
....
....
....
....
....

2 Heavy snow in north of England; motorists stranded; lambs buried in snow; half
a metre of snow overnight; electricity cut off; army called in; helicopters bring
supplies; elderly couple die; snow still falling.

....
....
....
....
....
....
....
....
....
....

3 President shot; comes out of hotel; young woman with gun; five shots; escapes into crowd; President hit in chest; three others wounded; taken to hospital; emergency operation; condition now satisfactory; big police hunt.

....

....

....

....

....

....

....

....

....

....

....

....

2 HEARSAY

You have heard that a friend of yours has had an accident, and although you have not seen him yourself, you have heard all the details. Someone asks you about it. Answer his questions, using the 'hearsay' expressions: **supposed to, apparently, I hear** and **I'm told**.

1 What's happened to George?
Apparently he's had a rather serious accident.

2 How did it happen?

....

3 Was it his fault?

....

4 Was anyone else hurt?

....

5 How is he getting on?

....

6 How is he feeling?

....

7 When will he be back at school/work?

....

⟫→

8 Where is he – at home or in hospital?

....

9 Can people go and visit him?

....

3 PASSIVE REPORTING VERBS

Little is known of the recluse millionaire Louis S. Denver III. Rewrite the information about him given below as in the example.

1 He was born in Manchester in 1932. (know)
He is known to have been born in Manchester in 1932.

2 His parents took him to America when he was seven. (think)

....

....

3 He is worth five billion dollars. (estimate)

....

4 He is living on a remote Greek island. (rumour)

....

....

5 He was responsible for several murders in the sixties. (allege)

....

....

6 He has been married five times. (believe)

....

7 He's a heavy drinker. (say)

....

8 He has had a serious heart attack recently. (think)

....

....

9 Several governments are suing him for tax offences. (report)

....

....

4 GOOD NEWS

Imagine a piece of really good news that you would like to read in a local or national newspaper. Write the story, including the headline and the details.

....
....
....
....
....
....
....
....
....
....
....
....
....
....
....
....
....
....
....
....

Revision crossword   Units 11–15

Across

1   Have you heard? .... there's been a big hotel fire in Los Angeles. (10)

7   ....'... certain to be an election before long. (6)

9   It was so cold last winter that the water in the lake .... (5)

11 .... they had done the shopping, they started to tidy up the flat. (5)

13 They're almost the same height. Jane is only .... taller than Robert. (8)

14 The director is .... to have stolen large amounts of company money, but nothing has yet been proved. (7)

15 When I .... finished with the book, I returned it to the library. (3)

16 About twenty thousand people .... estimated to have taken part in the demonstration. (3)

17 He didn't accept the invitation .... he had looked in his diary to see if he was free. (5)

20 Sugar .... in water. (9)

22 It was a miserable summer – it wasn't nearly as .... as it usually is. (3)

25 You should always test the temperature of the water before getting into the .... (4)

27 .... vegetables taste much better than tinned ones. (5)

28 It weighed almost nothing. It was as .... as a feather. (5)

29 Don't worry. There probably ....'... be any trouble. (4)

30 You have the best qualifications. You're .... to get the job. (4)

31 Comes back. (7)

34 .... expensive are taxis these days? (3)

36 Don't take the film out .... camera until you've turned the light out. (2,3)

38 If you carry on smoking you are .... get heart disease. (6,2)

41 Travelling by car isn't .... as travelling by plane. There are considerably more car accidents than there are plane crashes. (2,4)

42 I came as .... as I heard the news. (4)

43 When the alarm bell .... everyone left the building. (4)

44 Foolishly, he took the car on the road before he had had any driving .... (7)

Down

1 Horses aren't slow, but they can't run .... cheetahs can. (2,4,2)

2 .... that you don't get lost, it'll only take you about two hours to get there. (8)

3 He's very young. He's not .... as old as I'd thought he would be. (6)

4 I realised that I was going to be .... if I didn't hurry. (4)

5 You ....'... pay the bill until you've checked it. (8)

6 Incorrect. (5)

8 He is .... to be one of the richest men in the world. (4)

10 They were completely .... – they had been climbing the mountain for six days. (9)

12 As soon as I had .... the letter, I tore it up and threw it away. (4)

15 When you .... the gas, you put the coffee on the stove. (4,3)

18 I didn't even have time to unpack. ... . just come back from Italy when my boss sent me off to Spain. (1,3,4)

19 Houses in the country are a .... cheaper than they are in the city. (3)

21 You should book a seat in advance. .... you might not get a ticket. (9)

23 It is believed .... they are now living in Texas. (4)

24 .... the dog ran towards him, he jumped back into his car. (4)

26 .... had they got married than they started arguing. (2,6)

27 Computers are .... cheaper than they used to be. (3)

32 .... my salary is increased, I won't be able to afford a holiday this year. (6)

33 I wish I could .... without my glasses. (3)

34 I .... that he's getting another divorce. Is that true, do you know? (4)

35 I wouldn't buy one yet if I were you. The prices are .... to come down soon. (5)

37 You should .... off the mains before you change a fuse. (4)

39 Apples are 5p a .... more expensive than oranges. (4)

40 Oranges are slightly .... expensive than apples. (4)